MULTIPLY

A BIBLICAL GUIDE TO
INVESTING

DISCUSSION **GUIDE**

Sound Mind Investing
Financial Wisdom for Living Well

"Steady plodding brings prosperity; hasty speculation brings poverty."

- Proverbs 21:5 (TLB)

Multiply Discussion Guide
Copyright © 2019 by Sound Mind Investing

CONTENTS

WELCOME

For many people, investing feels complicated and intimidating.

It can seem *complicated* because of the unique language used by investors, such as "bull markets" and "bear markets," "asset allocation" and "exchange-traded funds." What does it all mean?

It can seem *intimidating* because of how quickly—and how far—the stock market can fall.

This study is designed to put your fears at rest and to equip you with the knowledge, confidence, and biblical foundation you need to invest successfully. It will give you essential information along with specific steps to profitably manage the money that's been entrusted to you. Ultimately, you'll be better equipped to provide for your family—now and in the future.

Throughout this study, you'll hear many references to retirement. Our intent is not to support the cultural idea of retirement as an extended time of leisure. In the Bible, there's just one reference to retirement and that pertained only to Levitical priests (Numbers 8:25)! Your entire life is to be lived in service to God, and your post-career days are when you may be able to have your greatest Kingdom impact. Our references to retirement are simply an acknowledgement that as you get older, your ability to earn income may decrease, so it's good stewardship to prepare financially for such a time.

If you complete all of the steps in this study, you will end up with a written investment plan tailored to your unique circumstances and goals. While it is our deep desire that this study will improve your experience with investing in very practical, tangible ways, that isn't our only objective.

Everything we do at Sound Mind Investing is motivated by a desire to glorify God and to encourage others to do likewise. After all, when Jesus was asked directly what matters most, he said, "Love the Lord your God with all your heart and with all your soul and with all your mind" (Matthew 22:37).

That's why each of the four sessions in this study contains questions designed to help you explore and more fully embrace God's teaching about money. The homework between sessions will encourage you to go deeper into God's Word, pray about how each topic applies to you, and memorize Scripture.

All of these exercises will help you take a truly biblical approach to investing. All are essential, not only for becoming more *effective* in your money management, but for becoming more *faithful* as well.

HOW TO GET THE MOST FROM THIS STUDY

Participate

If you're going through this study as part of a group (which we highly recommend), commit now to taking part in all four sessions. Your involvement every step of the way is crucial for two reasons. First, there's a lot of learning packed into each session. Miss just one session and you will have missed a lot. Second, life change occurs most effectively in community. You'll learn from and be encouraged by others in your group, just as they will learn from and be encouraged by you. You're in this together!

If you absolutely can't make it to one of the sessions, arrange to view that session's video segment on your own and work through the Discussion Guide content before the next session.

Take action

Between sessions, there will be some work to do—practical steps to take as well as Scripture to reflect on (and memorize!). Be sure to do this work. By putting the ideas you learn into action, you'll get the most value from this study.

BEFORE YOU BEGIN
PRE-WORK FOR SESSION 1

WELCOME TO THE MULTIPLY STUDY!

We're glad you're taking part in this four-session study about taking a biblical approach to investing.

In order to hit the ground running, please complete the following pre-work. It should just take you about 10 minutes to complete it.

1. On a scale of 1-to-10, with 1 being an "investing newbie" and 10 being an "experienced investor," where would you place yourself right now? Draw an "x" on the line. (We've all been "newbies" at some point, so it's OK to choose 1.)

INVESTING
NEWBIE   1   2   3   4   5   6   7   8   9   10   *EXPERIENCED*
                                                        INVESTOR

2. Think about your current investing situation—how knowledgeable you are about investing, how much you have invested, how much you're contributing to your investment account(s) each month, how you're choosing what to invest in, the results you're generating, etc. What aspect(s) of your investing situation would you most like to change and why?

3. Memorize the following verse before Session 1.

"Steady plodding brings prosperity; hasty speculation brings poverty."
- Proverbs 21:5 (TLB)

SESSION 1

WHO NEEDS THE STOCK MARKET?

KEY IDEA: To provide for your family over the long-term, you will need to set aside a portion of what you earn today and invest it wisely. For most people, the stock market provides the best investment opportunities.

DISCUSSION STARTER

Introduce yourself to others in your group. Then have each person take 30-60 seconds to summarize how they feel about investing. Are you knowledgeable and confident about investing? Intimidated by the stock market? Not certain how to invest? There are no right or wrong answers. Just say what comes most quickly to mind when you think about investing.

Part of the pre-work involved placing yourself somewhere on a 1-to-10 scale of investing experience, where 1 means you're an "investing newbie" and 10 means you're an "experienced investor." Where did you place yourself and why?

You were also asked to memorize Proverbs 21:5. Would two or three people recite that verse?

GROUP PRAYER

Before watching the video, pray as you feel led, perhaps thanking God that He brought each person to this study and asking Him to use the study to help everyone become better stewards of all that He has generously entrusted to your care.

VIDEO OUTLINE

(Keep this in front of you and take notes as you watch the Session 1 video.)

The Bible says a lot about money. An important example is found in the Parable of the Talents, where Jesus describes a wealthy person who entrusts his property to three servants while he is away.

> *"Again, it will be like a man going on a journey, who called his servants and entrusted his wealth to them." - Matthew 25:14*

One day the master returns to settle accounts with the three servants. Two of them doubled what was entrusted to them and the master had strong words of affirmation for them.

> *"His master replied, 'Well done, good and faithful servant! You have been faithful with a few things; I will put you in charge of many things. Come and share your master's happiness!'" - Matthew 25:21*

But the third servant was afraid of the master, so he hid what was entrusted to him and gave it back to the master upon his return. He didn't lose any of the money, but he didn't do anything productive with it either. Because of that, the master rebuked him.

> *"His master replied, 'You wicked, lazy servant!... you should have put my money on deposit with the bankers, so that when I returned I would have received it back with interest.'" - Matthew 25:26-27*

The Parable of the Talents shows the foundation of biblical money management. God is the creator and owner of everything. You are a steward, and it is your responsibility to manage God's resources faithfully, productively—to *multiply* them.

One of your specific stewardship responsibilities is to provide for your family.

> *"Anyone who does not provide for their relatives, and especially for their own household, has denied the faith and is worse than an unbeliever." - 1 Timothy 5:8*

Providing — Now and in the Future

While you're working, you provide for your family through your income. In order to *keep* providing for your family in your later years—in retirement—you'll have to set aside some of your income and manage that money in a way that makes it grow.

There are two key issues here:

- **Setting aside enough money**
- **Managing that money productively**

Realistically, your retirement could last for 20 years or more, which means you'll need to have a lot of money saved by the time you retire. In addition, old style pensions largely have been replaced with 401(k) plans, which means you're responsible for managing your retirement account.

Saving vs. Investing

A savings account is for short-term needs, such as emergency expenses. The rate of interest you earn on this money isn't what's most important. Safety and ease of access matter more.

An investment account is for long-term goals, such as retirement. With this money, because you won't need it for many years, you can afford to take calculated risks in order to pursue a higher rate of return.

Stock Market Essentials

While there are many ways to invest, for most people, the stock market offers the best opportunities.

A share of stock represents ownership in a company. The stock market is where shares of companies are bought and sold.

As you can see, the long-term returns from the stock market have been better than most other asset classes, such as bonds, gold, real estate, and cash, and they have been about three times higher than the inflation rate.[1]

Long-Term Average Annual Returns	
Stocks	10%
Bonds	5.5%
Gold	4.3%
Real Estate	3.8%
Cash	3.4%
Inflation	2.9%

Source: Stocks, bonds, cash, and inflation: Morningstar 1926-2017. Gold: Actual gold prices 1934-2017. Real Estate: Case Shiller Index 1926-2017.

[1] In Session 2, there will be more information about building a diversified portfolio.

'The Eighth Wonder of the World'

Albert Einstein reportedly described compounding as "the eighth wonder of the world." It is one of the most important concepts in investing.

To understand how compounding works, assume you invest $200 and earn 10% in each of the next two years. After the first year, you'll end up with $220. Your $200 will have earned 10%, or $20. The next year, you won't just earn another $20; you'll earn $22. That's because your original $200 will have earned 10% and so will the $20 you earned last year. That might not seem like a very big deal, but over time, the power of compounding can turn a little bit of money into a lot.

For example, let's say a 20-year-old investor named Claire invested $200 per month, kept at it for 50 years, and generated an average annual return of 7%[1]. At age 70, she will have invested $120,000. But because of her 7% average annual return, the power of compounding will have turned her $120,000 into nearly $1.1 million!

How to Maximize Compounding

The keys to Claire's success:

- **Consistent investing**
- **A good rate of return**
- **Time**

As the Bible says,

> *"Steady plodding brings prosperity; hasty speculation brings poverty."*
> *- Proverbs 21:5 (TLB)*

All three keys are important: Investing a portion of every dollar you earn, generating a good rate of return, and giving it time.

In Session 4, you'll learn how to figure out how much you should invest each month to meet your retirement goals.

[1]As we just saw, the long-term average annual return of the U.S. stock market has been 10%. We're using 7% in this example because it would be wise for Claire to make her portfolio less aggressive as she gets older (For example, moving from 100% stocks to 80% stocks/20% bonds and then 60% stocks/40% bonds), which would lower her potential returns.

To illustrate the importance of generating a good rate of return, let's compare Claire's results with those of her friend, Alex. He got started with investing when he was 20 years old as well. He also invested $200 per month and kept at it for 50 years. However, Alex chose more conservative investments, which generated a 6% average annual return, compared to the 7% Claire earned. As a result, at age 70, he ended up with $760,000—far less than the nearly $1.1 million Claire accumulated.

To illustrate the importance of time, let's look at another one of Claire's friends, William, who got off to a later start with investing. Beginning at age 30, he invested $200 per month and generated the same 7% average annual return that Claire generated. However, he paid a big price for his later start. While he invested just $24,000 less than Claire, he ended up with about $500,000 less.

No matter how old you are, the sooner you get the power of compounding working for you, the better.

GROUP DISCUSSION

1. What are some of your main takeaways from the video? What stood out to you?

2. People invest for a variety of reasons, but one of the most common investment goals is building a sufficient retirement nest egg. At what age do you see yourself retiring from full-time paid work and why did you choose that age?

3. What do you hope or plan to do in retirement? What type of Kingdom impact do you hope to have in that season of your life?

4. Do you think your expenses will go up or down in retirement? Why?

5. When you think about your sources of retirement income—Social Security, your retirement savings, maybe some form of continued work—how confident are you that you'll be able to cover your later life expenses and why?

6. In the pre-work, you were asked what aspect of your investing situation you would most like to change. What did you write down?

7. In the video, we looked at the Parable of the Talents, in which Jesus talks about a wealthy person who goes on a journey and entrusts his property to three servants. The property owner represents God and the servants represent us. The starting point of biblical money management is understanding that God is the creator and owner of everything and we are stewards (managers) of what's been entrusted to us. To what degree does that perspective guide your daily experience with money and in what ways?

GROUP PRAYER

Close your group time in prayer.

HOME WORK
Take it to Heart

One key lesson from the Parable of the Talents is that God is the creator and owner of everything, and you are a manager of all that has been temporarily entrusted to your care. To further reinforce God's ownership of everything, read the following verses:

"Yours, LORD, is the greatness and the power and the glory and the majesty and the splendor, for *everything in heaven and earth is yours.* Yours, LORD, is the kingdom; you are exalted as head over all. Wealth and honor come from you; you are the ruler of all things" - 1 Chr. 29:11-12, emphasis added.

"The earth is the LORD's, and everything in it, the world, and all who live in it; for he founded it on the seas and established it on the waters." - Psalm 24:1-2, emphasis added

"For all the animals of the forest are mine, and I own the cattle on a thousand hills. I know every bird on the mountains, and all the animals of the field are mine. If I were hungry, I would not tell you, for *all the world is mine and everything in it.*" - Psalm 50:10-12 (NLT), emphasis added

1. In what ways would your attitude about money–and your uses of money–change if you more fully saw all of the money you have as belonging to God instead of you? Try to list two or three examples.

2. Read and reflect on 1 Timothy 5:8, which emphasizes your responsibility to provide for your family. How confident are you that you are taking adequate steps today to provide for your family long-term? Circle your answer on the scale below.

| NOT AT ALL CONFIDENT | 1 2 3 4 5 6 7 8 9 10 | VERY CONFIDENT |

3. Take a few minutes to pray. If you haven't done so already, acknowledge God as the owner of everything in your life and accept your role as manager. Ask God to use this study to help you provide for your family long-term through wise investing.

Take Action

1. How much money do you have invested for the following purposes?

RETIREMENT

Account Type (IRA, 401K, Etc.): _____   Amount: $ _____

Account Type (IRA, 401K, Etc.): _____   Amount: $ _____

Account Type (IRA, 401K, Etc.): _____   Amount: $ _____

Account Type (IRA, 401K, Etc.): _____   Amount: $ _____

COLLEGE

529 Plan Account   Amount: $ _____

Other College Savings Account   Amount: $ _____

OTHER

Account Type: _____   Amount: $ _____

GRAND TOTAL

Total Invested in All Accounts: TOTAL: $ _____

2. How much are you contributing to your retirement account(s) each month?

$ _____

3. If applicable, how much are you saving for your kids' future college costs each month?

$ _____

4. How much are you contributing to any other investment account each month?

$ _____

5. What's the total amount you are investing each month and what percentage of your household's monthly gross income is that?

$ _____   _____ %

Pre-Work for Session 2

Please complete this pre-work before Session 2.

1. Which of the following investment risks are you most concerned about? Put a check mark next to the risk you think has the greatest potential to hinder your success as an investor.

☐ **Inflation Risk:** The cost of living could grow faster than the value of your retirement portfolio.

☐ **Longevity Risk:** You could outlive your money.

☐ **Market Risk:** You could lose money in the market.

☐ **The Risk of Getting in Your Own Way:** You could let your emotions get the best of you and make unwise decisions, such as selling investments out of fear.

2. Why did you choose that risk?

3. Memorize the following verse before Session 2.

> *"But the fruit of the Spirit is love, joy, peace, patience, kindness, good-ness, faithfulness, gentleness, self-control; against such things there is no law." - Galatians 5:22-23 (ESV)*

SESSION 2
MANAGING RISK

KEY IDEA: Although the long-term returns generated by the stock market are impressive, the ride can get rough from time to time. Knowing how to manage risk is essential to your success as an investor.

DISCUSSION STARTER

As pre-work for this session, you were asked which of four investment risks you are most concerned about: Inflation risk, longevity risk, market risk, and the risk of getting in your own way. Which one did you choose and why?

Would a couple of people recite the memory verses that were part of the pre-work, Galatians 5:22-23?

GROUP PRAYER

The video you're about to watch highlights four risks of stock market investing and offers practical steps you can take to manage those risks. Ultimately, though, a believer's protection is found in Christ. As the Bible says, "The name of the Lord is a fortified tower; the righteous run to it and are safe" (Proverbs 18:10). So, before watching the video, spend a few minutes in prayer, perhaps expressing that with investing—as with life in general—there are many uncertainties, but your trust is in God's protection and provision.

VIDEO OUTLINE

(Keep this in front of you and take additional notes as you watch Session 2.)

If you looked at a long-term chart of the U.S. stock market's performance, it would show an upward trend. But the path has not been smooth. There have been many ups and downs along the way. To be successful as an investor, you have to understand that investing comes with risk.

Here are several of the most common risks associated with investing, along with steps you can take to manage them.

1. Inflation Risk

Inflation risk is the possibility that the money you're setting aside for the future won't grow in value as fast as the cost of living. To manage this risk, choose investments that have a good track record of outpacing inflation over the long-haul, such as stocks.

2. Longevity Risk

Longevity risk is the possibility that you might outlive your money. Of course, you can't know for sure how many years you'll need your money to last because you don't know how long you'll live. The best way to manage this risk is to build your investment plan around the assumption of a long life. (We'll discuss how to develop a written investment plan in Session 4.)

3. Market Risk

Market risk is the ever-present possibility that the market—and your investments—will decline in value. One important way to manage this risk is to diversify your portfolio. It's a principle that comes straight from the pages of Scripture.

> *"Divide your investments among many places, for you do not know what risks might lie ahead."* – Ecclesiastes 11:2 (NLT)

Asset allocation is the thoughtful, intentional process of deciding *how* to diversify your portfolio. While there are many asset classes, such as stocks, bonds, real estate, precious metals, and more, *the starting point of asset allocation is deciding how to divide your portfolio between stocks and bonds.*

When you buy a share of stock, you become a part owner of a company. If the company does well, your stock should become more valuable.

When you buy a bond, you become a lender. The issuer of the bond, such as a corporation, city, or the federal government, is borrowing money from you. As long as the bond issuer doesn't go bankrupt, it will repay the money along with some interest.

Generally, stocks have greater growth potential than bonds, but they are also riskier. Stocks should help your portfolio grow, whereas bonds should help reduce volatility.

Your Optimal Asset Allocation

Your best mix of stocks and bonds is determined by:

1. Your investing temperament, or risk tolerance
2. Your investing time frame

According to the widely accepted "rules" of asset allocation, the younger you are, the more your stock/bond mix should tilt toward stocks. You have time to ride out the market's ups and downs in pursuit of greater gains. As you get closer to retirement, you should play it safer, decreasing your exposure to stocks and increasing your bond holdings.

Mutual Funds

Another important way to diversify is to invest in mutual funds instead of individual stocks and bonds.

A mutual fund pools money from many investors and invests it in many stocks or other investments. For example, an S&P 500 index fund invests in approximately 500 large U.S. companies. Buying just a single share, which you can do for less than $100, will diversify your money across hundreds of businesses representing many different sectors of the economy.

An exchange-traded fund, or ETF, is a type of mutual fund. It, too, pools money from many investors and invests it in many different stocks or other investments. The main difference is how you buy and sell ETFs. You'll find more details at www.smind.co/multiply.

So, how do you manage market risk?

1. Build a portfolio based on your optimal asset allocation
2. Invest in mutual funds instead of individual stocks and bonds

4. The Risk of Getting in Your Own Way

This may be the single biggest threat to your success as an investor. Making investment decisions based on emotions, such as fear, usually does more harm than good.

One way to avoid emotional decision-making is to see yourself as a long-term investor. It can help to know a little market history.

Taking the Long View

Over the past 100 years, here's how often the stock market has generated a positive return based on various time periods.

One-day periods: 54%
One-month periods: 62%
One-year periods: 79%
10-year periods: 94%
20-year periods: 100%
Source: Returns 2.0

In other words, if you look at all of the individual days the market has been open over the past 100 years, it has generated a positive return just better than half the time. But the longer the time period, the more likely it is that the market has been positive. Put another way, the longer you stay invested in the market and weather the short-term ups and downs, the better your chances of generating a positive return.

Here's one more bit of helpful market history. Of all the bull markets and bear markets since 1926, bull markets have lasted longer than bear markets and they've added more value than bear markets have taken away.

That isn't to say that market declines are easy to take, but they're *easier* to take when you understand that the market moves in cycles and time is on your side.

GROUP DISCUSSION

1. What are some of your takeaways from the video? What stood out to you?

2. Think about the impact of inflation. What examples can you think of that show how significantly inflation has driven the cost of various items upward? What's a product or service you buy regularly that you can recall costing a lot less in the past?

3. In Session 1, you were asked at what age you think you will retire. Now think about how long you might live. If your estimates turn out to be correct, how many years does that mean you will spend in retirement?

4. Do you know anyone who worked his or her whole life only to retire without enough money to live on? Tell a little bit about that person's story.

5. Another risk discussed was *market risk*. What was the approach suggested on the video for managing market risk and what are some practical ways to implement that approach?

6. The fourth risk was *the risk of getting in your own way,* usually by reacting emotionally to significant changes in the market. How well have you done at managing your emotions during past market downturns?

7. Some of the risks talked about in this session can be managed by taking certain practical steps, such as diversifying your investments and incorporating the assumption of a long life into your investment plan. But one of the risks, the risk of getting in your own way, has a lot to do with your temperament and emotions. Specifically, being impatient can lead you to take on too much risk and being fearful can lead you to be too conservative.

If an investor is impatient, wanting his or her investments to increase in value more quickly than might be realistic, what deeper spiritual issue could be at work?

8. If someone is fearful, wanting to exit the market at the first sign of trouble, what deeper spiritual issue could be at work?

9. Which of those tendencies—impatience or fear—is a bigger issue for you? In what ways has it impacted you—whether in your investing or otherwise?

GROUP PRAYER

Close your group time in prayer.

HOMEWORK
Take it to Heart

In this session's video, you heard about the importance of taking the long view with your investments. The Bible describes patience as a "fruit of the Spirit" (Galatians 5:22-23), and it also cautions, "...a person who wants quick riches will get into trouble" (Proverbs 28:20 NLT).

1. How difficult is it for you to be patient (with your investments, or generally)? Why do you think that is?

2. If patience is a challenge for you, spend time reading and reflecting on God's patience (2 Peter 3:9, Romans 15:5, 1 Timothy 1:16). Then spend time praying, asking God to help you get at the source of your impatience and asking Him to cultivate in you greater patience.

3. Another "fruit of the Spirit" described in the Bible is peace. And yet, in the video you also heard that one of the greatest risks you face as an investor is allowing fear to guide your investment decisions. To what degree do you wrestle with fear (with your investments or generally)? Why do you think that is?

4. If fear is an issue for you as an investor, here are three ways to keep it from getting the best of you:

- **Learn About Market History**
  As described on the video, it's normal for the market to cycle between bull markets and bear markets, but bull markets usually last longer than bear markets and add more value than bear markets take away. In other words, market declines are normal. You should expect them from time to time and not be overly concerned about them.

- **Use a Trustworthy Investment Strategy**
  This is a topic that will be covered in more detail in Session 4.

- **Have Faith**
  If you've been praying about your investment decisions, have sought godly counsel, and have tried to understand and apply biblical teaching to your investments, all of that should give you some peace of mind. Still, it can help to read, reflect on, and memorize verses such as:

> *"Have I not commanded you? Be strong and courageous. Do not be frightened, and do not be dismayed, for the Lord your God is with you wherever you go." - Joshua 1:9 (ESV)*

> *"Give all your worries and cares to God, for he cares about you." - 1 Peter 5:7 (NLT)*

As you think about your finances in general and your investments in particular, spend time in prayer, taking any fears or concerns you have to God, asking Him to ease your mind and give you what you need in order to manage money wisely and with peace of mind.

Take Action

1. Before making any decisions about specific investments, it's essential that you know your optimal asset allocation. Use the "Your Optimal Asset Allocation" process found at www.smind.co/multiply.

2. What is your optimal asset allocation?

    _____% stocks and _____% bonds

3. In Session 4, you'll learn about the importance of using an objective *process* for choosing investments. For now, think about how you're currently choosing investments. Write a short statement that explains how you're making those decisions. Explain why you chose the specific mutual funds or other investments you have right now.

4. Would you say your approach to choosing investments is more *subjective* (based on gut feel or someone's opinions or predictions) or *objective* (a fact- and rules-based process)?

SUBJECTIVE ——————————————————— *OBJECTIVE*
1   2   3   4   5   6   7   8   9   10

5. How well could you explain to a middle school student what you've chosen to invest in and why?

NOT WELL ——————————————————— *VERY WELL*
1   2   3   4   5   6   7   8   9   10

6. What's your portfolio's track record? Has it been delivering the sort of returns you need?

BAD TRACK RECORD ——————————————————— *GOOD TRACK RECORD*
1   2   3   4   5   6   7   8   9   10

7. When the market gets volatile, do you rest easy, knowing your investments are well-positioned for long-term growth, or does it make you wonder whether you're investing in the best way? In other words, how confident are you about staying with your approach to investing even in bear markets?

NOT CONFIDENT ——————————————————— *VERY CONFIDENT*
1   2   3   4   5   6   7   8   9   10

Pre-Work for Session 3

Please complete this pre-work before Session 3.

1. Which retirement investing vehicle, if any, are you using?

☐ **401k**   ☐ **IRA**   ☐ **Both**

2. Why?

3. Which type of 401(k) or IRA are you using?

☐ **Traditional**   ☐ **Roth**   ☐ **Both**

4. Why?

5. Memorize the following verse before Session 3.

"If any of you lacks wisdom, you should ask God, who gives generously to all without finding fault, and it will be given to you." – James 1:5

SESSION 3

THE LEAST TAXING WAY TO INVEST

KEY IDEA: There are ways to invest that will enable you to save on taxes. While this may sound like a complicated topic, just two key decisions are needed in order to make use of the tax-advantaged accounts best suited to your unique situation.

DISCUSSION STARTER

One of the action steps from Session 2 was to figure out your optimal asset allocation. Did you do that? If so, how did it turn out?

Who can recite the memory verse from last week, James 1:5? (Have at least two people do this.)

GROUP PRAYER

The video you're about to watch is a bit technical. It walks you through two key decisions that'll help you invest in the most tax-advantaged way. So, before watching the video, take some time to pray. You may want to pray for patience! More importantly, ask God to use this session to guide each participant to the best possible decisions.

VIDEO OUTLINE

(Keep this in front of you and take notes as you watch. For this session, the Video Outline includes some questions with spaces where you can fill in your answers. Feel free to answer the ones you can easily answer while the video is playing, but don't worry if you *can't* answer some of them. In the Take Action section, you'll be directed back to this content so you can take your time in answering all of the questions.)

We all have to pay our taxes. It's the law, and it's our biblical responsibility.

> *"Give to everyone what you owe them: If you owe taxes, pay taxes; if revenue, then revenue; if respect, then respect; if honor, then honor."*
> *- Romans 13:7*

But you don't have to *overpay*, and part of good stewardship is making use of the tax-advantaged investment tools available to you. Doing so boils down to two key decisions.

Your First Decision: Which Investment Vehicle to Use—a 401(k) Plan or an IRA?

- Do you have access to a 401(k) or other workplace retirement account?

☐ Yes ☐ No

If not, your path is clear. Use an IRA to invest for your later years.

- If you do have access to a workplace plan, will your employer match your contributions?

☐ Yes ☐ No

Such contributions usually have two components. First is the *amount* of the match. Your employer might contribute 25 cents to your retirement plan for each dollar you contribute, or even a dollar for every dollar you contribute.

Second is the *percentage of your salary* the match will pertain to. For example, your employer might contribute 50 cents for every dollar you contribute *up to six percent of your salary*. In that scenario, if your salary is $5,000 per month and you contribute 10% ($500) to your retirement plan, your employer would contribute $150 (6% of your salary is $300; a 50 cent match on each of those dollars totals $150).

- If your company offers a match, how much money will it contribute for every dollar you contribute?

☐ **25 Cents**   ☐ **50 Cents**   ☐ **$1**

☐ **Different Amount: $_____**

Any match is a great deal. At very least, try to invest as much as is needed to get the full match offered by your employer.

- If your employer offers a match on 401(k) contributions you make, are you contributing enough to get the full match?

☐ **Yes** ☐ **No**

Still, you probably need to invest more to meet your retirement goals. If that's your situation, your next decision is whether to invest more in your workplace retirement plan or use an IRA for these additional investments instead. In part, that decision depends on your answer to the next question.

- Are you eligible to make tax-advantaged contributions to an IRA?

☐ **Yes** ☐ **No**

If you are covered by a 401(k), then whether you are allowed to contribute to an IRA, and if so, how much of a tax benefit you'll receive, depends on your income. If you don't know if you are eligible, check the IRA eligibility rules at www.smind.co/multiply.

If you're *not* eligible, your only choice for additional tax-advantaged retirement investing is to invest more in your workplace 401(k) plan.

If you *are* eligible, where you should make these additional contributions depends, in part, on how satisfied you are with the investment choices available through your workplace plan.

- Are you satisfied with your 401(k) plan's investment options? In other words, do they enable you to invest as you would like to invest?

☐ **Yes** ☐ **No**

If you *are* satisfied with the investment choices available through your 401(k) plan, contribute more money there. That'll keep things simple.

If you *aren't* satisfied with those choices, use an IRA for your additional contributions. An IRA will give you access to a wide range of investment options.

Up to this point, we've been discussing your options assuming you have access to a 401(k) plan and your employer offers a match on some of your contributions. But **what if there's no match?**

If you have access to a 401(k) plan, but your employer does *not* offer a match on your contributions, you may want to make an IRA the starting point for your retirement investing and then make any needed additional contributions to your workplace plan.

While the amount you can contribute to an IRA may be less than what you can contribute to a 401(k) plan, keep this in mind: If you are married, both you and your spouse should be able to contribute to an IRA, even if your spouse doesn't work outside the home.

Your Second Decision: Which Type of IRA or 401(k) to Use—Traditional or Roth?

Once you've decided which retirement *vehicle* to use (a 401(k) or an IRA), your second key decision is which *type*: A *traditional* or a *Roth* 401(k) or IRA.

A traditional account provides an upfront tax deduction for the money you contribute. Money in the account (contributions and earnings) is then **tax-deferred**—it's taxed when you withdraw it years later.

With a Roth account, it works the other way around. There is no tax deduction for contributions. However, you can withdraw money from the account **tax-free** in retirement.

(Roth accounts have several other unique benefits, which you can read about at www.smind.com/multiply.)

Which one is best for you? Generally, if you are in a relatively low tax bracket now (such as if you are early in your career) but expect to be in a higher tax bracket in retirement, a Roth will likely be more advantageous to you. If you are further along in your career and in a relatively high tax bracket now, you may be better served by a traditional IRA or 401(k).

But this is **not an either/or decision.** To diversify your tax liability, you could use both types of accounts.

Other Considerations

Remember, 401(k) plans and IRAs are *retirement* accounts. Withdrawing money from them before retirement can be costly. Money borrowed or withdrawn from retirement savings is not growing to meet your future needs, and in some cases, an early withdrawal will cost you in the form of a penalty and taxes.

When you leave an employer, it's generally best to transfer ("roll over") the money from your workplace retirement plan to an IRA. If that's what you decide to do, have the custodian that will hold the IRA handle the transaction so you don't end up owing any penalties or taxes.

GROUP DISCUSSION

This was a fairly technical session, and sometimes topics like this can seem confusing or overwhelming. But keep in mind two points made in Scripture:

First, God has given you a sound mind with which to successfully navigate decisions such as the ones discussed in this session. (Someone read 2 Timothy 1:7.)

Second, God promises to give you wisdom just for the asking. (Someone read James 1:5.)

1. What are your main takeaways from the video? What stood out to you?

2. Let's go over some of the main points from the video to make sure we all understand them. The first point was that there are two key decisions to make related to tax-advantaged investing: Which investment *vehicle* to use for retirement investing (IRA or 401k) and which *type* (traditional or Roth). Who can explain some of the main differences between an IRA and a 401(k)?

3. What about traditional vs. Roth? Who can explain some of the key differences between those *types* of retirement accounts?

4. If you are currently investing for your later years, which vehicle are you using—a workplace plan, such as a 401(k) plan, an IRA, or both? Why?

5. Which *type* of account are you using—traditional, Roth, or both—and why?

6. What next step does each person feel prompted to take based on the content of this session?

7. Have you ever prayed over decisions like the ones discussed in this session? If not, why? (Allow time for a couple of people to answer). Let's do that right now.

GROUP PRAYER

Close your group time in prayer.

HOMEWORK
Take it to Heart

These decisions—401(k) or IRA, traditional or Roth—are important. Choosing well is part of good stewardship and will have a significant impact on your future financial situation. So, pray for patience, wisdom, and good decision-making.

As discussed in Session 1, the sooner you get the power of compounding returns working for you, the better. However, finding the money to contribute to a workplace retirement plan or IRA may be a challenge. If that's your situation, pray about this as well, asking God to help you find ways to free up money to set aside for your future.

1. What are some ideas that come to mind?

Take Action

1. Go back through the Video Outline, taking the time to more completely answer the questions. The more knowledgeable you are about your workplace retirement plan or your IRA options, the better.

2. To help answer questions, such as whether you qualify to make tax-advantaged contributions to an IRA, and to further explore whether a traditional or Roth account makes the most sense for you, use the resources at www.smind.co/multiply.

3. If your company offers a 401(k) plan and you're interested in a Roth account, find out whether your company offers that option. If so, find out how to take advantage of it. If not, ask if a Roth option is something your company could offer in the future.

4. If you don't have access to a workplace retirement plan, investigate opening an Individual Retirement Account with a brokerage firm such as Fidelity, E-Trade, Schwab, Vanguard, or TD Ameritrade. Most discount brokers don't charge fees for IRAs, and they typically offer a large number of mutual funds from which to choose. There's more guidance about choosing a good broker at www.smind.co/multiply.

5. Also online, you'll find an Investment Plan template. You don't need to start filling it out just yet, but print it and bring it to the next session.

Pre-Work for Session 4

Please complete this pre-work before Session 4.

1. Which of the following approaches to choosing investments are you currently taking?

   ☐ **DIY**
     ☐ Self-selected index funds
     ☐ Target-date fund

   ☐ **DIY with help (Investment Newsletter)**

   ☐ **Advisor**

   ☐ **Other / Describe:**

2. Are you satisfied with the investment approach you're using?

   ☐ Yes   ☐ No

3. If not, what changes are you considering?

4. Memorize the following verse before Session 4.

   "Moreover, it is required of stewards that they be found faithful."
   - 1 Corinthians 4:2 (ESV)

SESSION 4
PUTTING IT ALL TOGETHER

KEY IDEA: Creating a written investment plan that describes your long-term financial goals and investment strategy will help you make better investment decisions. It also will give you a steady reference point during market storms.

DISCUSSION STARTER

Part of your pre-work for this session involved indicating whether you're satisfied with the investment approach you're using right now, and if not, writing down some changes you're considering. What, if anything, did you write down?

You were also encouraged to look into whether your company offers a Roth 401(k) option (if you're interested in that) or investigate opening an IRA (if you don't have access to a workplace retirement plan). Did you take either of these steps? If so, talk about what you learned or what you did.

Lastly, would a couple of people recite the memory verse, 1 Corinthians 4:2?

GROUP PRAYER

Toward the end of the video you're about to watch, you will be introduced to three different approaches for choosing specific investments. Before watching, take some time to pray. Consider asking God to show each participant the best approach for their household.

VIDEO OUTLINE

(This session will walk you through the development of an investment plan using a hypothetical couple, "the Browns." Take notes on this outline, or if you find it more helpful, write notes on your Investment Plan template.)

Creating a written investment plan is important for four reasons:

1. Planning is affirmed in Scripture

> *"The plans of the diligent lead to profit as surely as haste leads to poverty." - Proverbs 21:5*

2. A written plan will help you think through and make the best investment decisions

3. If you're married, writing a plan together will foster communication and teamwork

4. A written plan will help you stay on track, especially when the market gets volatile

Essential Elements of a Good Investment Plan (*The Browns' Example*)

CURRENT SITUATION

In the first section of your investment plan, you describe your current circumstances.

Age(s):
Mike and Mary Brown are both 32 and have two children, ages 4 and 2.

Annual Income:
$81,000. Mike works full-time, earning $72,000. Mary works part-time, earning $9,000.

Current retirement savings:
$120,000.

Current monthly contributions to retirement accounts:
$800. Mike automatically contributes 9% of his salary ($540), his company contributes 50 cents for every dollar Mike contributes up to 6% of his salary ($180), and Mary automatically contributes $80 per month to a Roth IRA.

The Browns also put $100 per month into college savings accounts for each of their kids.

(Automation is a great tool for helping you meet your investment goals. Most workplace retirement plans allow for automatic contributions from each of your paychecks. If you're using an IRA, automation should be available as well, but you'll have to set it up. It is highly recommended.)

GOALS

In this section, you describe your investing objectives.

Like many people, the Browns' primary investment goal is to build a large enough nest egg to be able to retire when they're older. While they're planning to work until age 70, they're building some margin into their plan just in case they're not able to work that long. So, their investment plan is built around an assumption of retiring at age 67.

Also, they'd like to be able to cover at least half the cost of a state college for each of their kids.

OPTIMAL ASSET ALLOCATION

In this section, you write down the stock/bond allocation you'll use in your investment portfolio. You should have this information from Session 2. (Refer back to the Take Action section.)

Primarily due to their young age, the Browns' optimal asset allocation is 100% stocks.

RUN SOME NUMBERS

Now use one of the retirement-planning calculators recommended on the Sound Mind Investing website (www.smind.co/multiply) to estimate how much you should accumulate by the time you retire, determine whether you're on track, and consider what you could change if you're not on track.

The calculator the Browns used required just six pieces of information:

1. **Age:** The Browns are both 32
2. **Income:** $81,000
3. **Current retirement savings:** $120,000
4. **Monthly contributions to retirement accounts:** $800
5. **Retirement standard of living:** The Browns think they may spend less money in retirement than they do now. (The calculator takes inflation into account.)
6. **Investment style:** Since the Browns' optimal asset allocation is 100% stocks, they chose "Most Aggressive"

The calculator then lets you know whether you're on track. The Browns were surprised to see they're *not* on track.

ADJUSTMENTS

Now use the calculator to identify and make changes that will enable you to more effectively prepare for retirement.

For example, the calculator automatically set the Browns' life expectancy at 93. But they want to be more conservative than that and changed it to 95. At first, that made it appear that they were *less* on track. However, making other adjustments, such as pushing back their intended retirement age and increasing how much they save each month, improved their picture.

INVESTMENTS

In this section, you describe how you've chosen to invest.

The key to making good investments is choosing a good investment *strategy*. There are four hallmarks of such a strategy:

1. It is driven by an *objective* investment selection process (i.e., it follows clear, unbiased rules)
2. It is easy to understand
3. It has a successful track record
4. It is emotionally acceptable to you. That means two things. First, you're willing to do what it takes to execute the strategy; and second, you're comfortable sticking with the strategy no matter what's happening in the stock market.

How can you find such a strategy? Here are some options.

Three Investment Approaches

Each of the following investment approaches has the *potential* to provide you with a strategy that meets the four criteria just listed.

1. DIY (do it yourself)

There are two relatively simple ways you could take a do-it-yourself approach to investing and incorporate a trustworthy investment strategy.

A. Build a portfolio with index funds.

You could build a portfolio with index funds that spread your dollars across stocks and bonds according to your optimal asset allocation. Here are some examples.

Funds	Optimal Asset Allocation		
	100% Stocks	80% Stocks / 20% Bonds	60% Stocks/40% Bonds
Total U.S. Stock Fund*	80%	64%	48%
Total International Stock Fund**	20%	16%	12%
Total Bond Market Fund***	0%	20%	40%

*Examples of total U.S. stock funds include Vanguard's VTSAX, Fidelity's FSKAX, and Schwab's SWTSX

**Examples of total international funds include Vanguard's VTIAX, Fidelity's FZILX, and Schwab's SWISX

***Examples of total bond market funds include Vanguard's VBTLX, Fidelity's FTBFX, and Schwab's SWAGX

B. Use a target-date fund.

An even easier approach is to use a target-date fund. With a target-date fund, you simply choose a fund with the year closest to the date of your intended retirement as part of its name. For example, if you plan to retire around the year 2060, you could buy shares of the Fidelity Freedom 2060 Fund or the Vanguard Target-Retirement 2060 Fund. Many mutual fund companies offer target-date funds.

While choosing your own index funds would be a little more time consuming than using a target-date fund, the advantages are that you *may* be able to reduce your costs (the expense ratios[1] of the index funds you choose may be lower than the expense ratio of a target-date fund) and you would gain more flexibility in managing your stock/bond allocation if you would like to do so.

Here's how both of these DIY investment approaches—choosing your own index funds or using a target-date fund—meet the four criteria of a trustworthy investment strategy described earlier.

Objectivity. Both approaches follow the rules of asset allocation. If you have a long time until retirement, you would have most, if not all, of your portfolio in stocks. On the other hand, if you plan to retire relatively soon, you may have 60 percent of your portfolio allocated to stocks and 40 percent to bonds and cash.

Easy to understand. As just described, the rules of asset allocation are very straight-forward.

Solid track record. As you may expect, an 80/20 stock/bond allocation will do better in a growing market than a 60/40 allocation. By the same token, a 60/40 allocation will hold up better in a decline than an 80/20 portfolio.

(On the Resources page at www.smind.co/multiply, you'll find links to the historical performance of index fund portfolios using different asset allocations and to various companies' target-date fund pages, which will describe how their portfolios are allocated and how they have performed. Also, you will find more information about the pros and cons of target-date funds.)

Emotional acceptability. Both of these DIY approaches easily meet the first standard of emotional acceptability in that they require very little work on your part. That's especially true with a target-date fund. Just choose the fund best suited to your investment time frame and it will have made the asset allocation decisions for you. As you get older, it will even automatically adjust its asset allocation, making it increasingly conservative.

Whether you're comfortable sticking with either of these approaches no matter what happens in the market is largely about expectations management. In a growing market, each one only has the potential to *match* (not exceed) the market's return, and it will only do so to the degree that it has your portfolio invested in stocks. In a declining market, the only defensive mechanism built into each approach is its allocation to bonds and cash.

The next two investing approaches make use of professional guidance, which *may* enable you to *outperform* the market, gaining more than the market during bull markets and better protecting you against loss during bear markets.

[1] There's more information about mutual fund expenses, such as expense ratios, at www.smind.co/multiply

Using an advisor—via either of the following two approaches—can be especially helpful during times of market stress, when a voice of reason can help you stay on track.

2. DIY, With Help

This approach involves subscribing to an investment newsletter that offers specific investment strategies and investment recommendations. With this approach, you would invest your money through a broker, such as Fidelity or Schwab, and then make the investments recommended by the newsletter. This can be a relatively low-cost way to avail yourself of professional investment guidance. Some investment newsletters charge as little as $99 per year. As you consider subscribing to an investment newsletter, make sure its strategies meet the four criteria discussed earlier.

3. Advisor-Managed

A third investment approach is to work with a financial advisor. In this scenario, you would turn your portfolio over to an advisor. After getting to know your circumstances and goals, the advisor would manage your portfolio in a way that he or she believes is best suited to you.

While this is the most customized approach to investing, it is also the most expensive. Many advisors charge a fee amounting to 1% or more of the value of your portfolio. Many also require that you have at least $100,000 or $250,000 for them to manage.

The Browns' Approach

The Browns chose to use a target-date fund in Mike's 401(k) plan since the plan's investment choices are fairly limited. For Mary's IRA, they chose to follow the advice of an investment newsletter. They like to be fairly hands-on with their investments but liked the idea of getting professional investment advice at a relatively low cost.

For their college investments, they chose to use a 529 plan, using the plan's pre-set age-based portfolios, which operate much like target-date funds.

MARKET EVENTS

In this final section of your written investment plan, you describe how you will respond to significant changes in the stock market. It is far better to think this through ahead of time than to respond emotionally in the moment.

Ideally, you would write down that you will not make any changes. That would be the clearest indication that you have chosen a trustworthy investment strategy. As described earlier, one of the four elements of such a strategy is that it's emotionally acceptable to you. In part, that means you're willing to stay with it in good times and bad.

There's an example of a Market Events statement at www.smind.co/multiply.

GROUP DISCUSSION

1. On the video, we heard that the key to knowing *what to invest in* is having a *trustworthy investment strategy*—that such a strategy will point to the best investments. What are your thoughts about that? How does it compare to the usual way people choose investments?

2. Of the three *approaches* to investing—do it yourself; do it yourself with the help of an investment newsletter; and work with an advisor—which one do you prefer and why?

3. Another point made on the video was that when the market gets volatile, you'll know you have a good strategy if you're comfortable not making any changes to your portfolio. During past times of market volatility, how comfortable have you been staying the course?

4. In Luke 16:11, we read these words from Jesus: "If you have not been trustworthy in handling worldly wealth, who will trust you with true riches?" What do you think He meant by "true riches"? In what ways has this study helped you incorporate your faith into your investing so that you're not just able to be more *effective* as an investor but more *faithful* as well?

5. As you think back on all four sessions of this study, what practical lessons or recommendations have been most helpful to you? What steps have you taken? And what spiritual lessons have been most helpful?

6. What are your most important next steps with your investments?

7. What prayer requests do you have, either related to your investing or your finances in general?

GROUP PRAYER

Close your group time in prayer.

HOMEWORK
Take it to Heart

Sound Mind Investing founder Austin Pryor was once asked why he named his company using the words and ideas from 2 Timothy 1:7. He explained that when he was on staff with a ministry called Cru[2], one of the popular handouts used in staff training was "The Paul Brown Letter," written by Cru Founder Bill Bright. Here's a relevant excerpt:

> Now you may ask, "What is the 'Sound-Mind Principle' of Scripture?" In 2 Timothy 1:7 we are told that *"God has not given us the spirit of fear; but of power, and of love and of a sound mind."* The sound mind referred to in this verse means a well-balanced mind: a mind that is under the control of Holy Spirit, "remade" according to Romans 12:1-2.
>
> There is a vast difference between the inclination of the natural or carnal man to use "common sense" and that of the spiritual man to follow the "Sound-Mind Principle." One, for understanding, depends upon the wisdom of man without benefit of God's wisdom and power; the latter, having the mind of Christ, receives wisdom and guidance from God moment by moment through faith.
>
> Are your decisions based on unpredictable emotions and chance circumstances, the "common sense" of the natural man? Or do you make your decisions according to the "Sound-Mind Principle" of Scripture?

"My thinking in 1990," Austin explained, "was that the verse not only points out the Resource we have as Christians to make Spirit-led decisions, but also mentions fear (which many have when it comes to investing and which we hope to help them overcome), as well as self-control or self-discipline (which is a requisite for successful investing)."

1. Take a few minutes right now to pray, asking God to help you implement the ideas from this study with a sound mind, using your God-given self-control to select and follow a trustworthy, objective investment strategy with the confidence and peace of mind that comes from faith in Christ.

[2] https://www.cru.org/

Take Action

1. Take your time re-reading this session's Video Outline, as it has more information than what was covered in the video.

2. Check each one of the following statements that is true for you:

   ☐ I have set my retirement age.

   ☐ I know my optimal asset allocation.

   ☐ I have used a retirement planning calculator to figure out approximately how much I will need to have in my investment account(s) by the time I retire.

   ☐ I know how much I need to invest each month.

   ☐ I'm investing that much each month.

   ☐ I have chosen my investment approach.
      ☐ DIY
      ☐ DIY with the help of an investment newsletter
      ☐ Advisor
      ☐ Other

   ☐ I'm using an investment strategy that is objective, easy to understand, has a good track record, and is emotionally acceptable to me.

3. Now review the statements that are not checked. What next step(s) should you take on your investing journey?

4. If you haven't done so already, print the Investment Plan template found at www.smind.co/multiply, fill it out (if you're married, complete the plan together), and then put your plan into action.

5. If you think working with an advisor might be helpful, two good resources for finding an advisor who shares your biblical worldview are:

   A. www.smiprivateclient.com
   B. www.kingdomadvisors.com

6. Go to www.smind.co/multiply and then download and print the report, "7 Key Principles for Christian Investing." Use this as a devotional in the coming weeks, reading and reflecting on it as you put the ideas from this study into practice.

FACILITATOR'S GUIDE

Read Before the First Session

Thank you for agreeing to facilitate this study! The Bible says more about money and material things than any subject other than the Kingdom of Heaven. Clearly, this is an important topic!

Of course, money is something we all deal with every day, and the Bible provides practical guidance on topics such as saving, debt, investing, spending, and more. However, as important as it is to live within our means and take other practical, productive financial steps, there's much more at stake here than saving for retirement. The Bible cautions, "For the love of money is a root of all kinds of evil. Some people, eager for money, have wandered from the faith and pierced themselves with many griefs" (1 Timothy 6:10).

So, pray regularly for your group, even before your group is fully formed. Pray that God will lead just the right people to the group and that the group will quickly become a safe place to talk about this most personal of topics. Commit to praying each week for each member of your group. Ask God to do a mighty work in the lives of each participant, including you!

How to Conduct a Multiply Study

Feel free to use the Multiply materials in whatever way best suits your needs. Here are the two most common ways the materials are used:

Small group. In this format, participants meet in someone's home or at church. They watch the videos together and a facilitator guides the group in their discussion. The ideal size is 8-12 participants.

Workshop. In this format, a room—typically in a church—is set up with round tables that each can seat 8-10 participants. A single facilitator could lead from the front of the room, managing the video, asking questions to be discussed at each table, and keeping the sessions running on time. If you use this format, be careful how you move from one question to the next. It can be helpful to allow a specific amount of time for each question and then announce when people have 60 seconds to wrap up their current discussion before moving on to the next questions.

Or, if you have enough volunteers, consider having a facilitator at each table. The facilitator at the front of the room would open the session, run the video, and keep things running on time. The table facilitators would manage the Discussion Starter and Group Discussion, and then close the session in prayer. The facilitator in the front of the room would then remind everyone about the homework and dismiss the session.

If you're going to use multiple facilitators—one at the front of the room and one at each table—decide who is going to send emails to participants in between sessions. We recommend that the table facilitators do this. Consider having a form on each table at Session 1 where participants can write their email address.

Whichever way you plan to facilitate, watch the video before each session so you know what's coming. And even though you're the facilitator, participate in the study, joining in the conversation and completing the work in between sessions.

Note that each session is designed to last 60-90 minutes, including the 13-18 minutes it will take to watch the video. If your meeting time is on the shorter side of that range, you'll need to be especially proactive in managing the Group Discussion time.

Review the discussion questions ahead of time and make sure you know which ones you want to be sure to use if you don't have time for all of them. During the video time, encourage people to take notes.

Keep in mind that you don't have to be a financial expert to serve your group well. You don't need to know the answer to every question. Mostly, your role is to *facilitate*, keeping conversation flowing, making sure the meetings run on time, encouraging the people in your group, and trusting in God's guidance.

FACILITATING SESSION 1:
WHO NEEDS THE STOCK MARKET?

The Big Idea

With all the confusing terminology associated with investing, and the potential to lose money during scary downturns, it can be tempting to avoid investing altogether. However, because of longer lifespans, many of us will spend 20-30 years in retirement, needing something other than a salary to live on. By setting aside a portion of all that you earn today and investing it wisely, you will be well prepared to provide for your family's long-term needs—thus, fulfilling your biblical responsibility.

Facilitation Tips

As you welcome people to the start of this four-week study, acknowledge that investing can be a tough topic. Assure the participants they will not be required to reveal personal details of their financial situation, emphasizing to them that what is said in the group is designed to stay within the group. There is an expectation of confidentiality. The group is intended to be a safe place where people feel heard. In fact, it's best to resist the temptation to give advice. Far better to take in the teaching on each session's video segment, truly listen to each other during each session's discussion time, make sure everyone completes the action steps in between sessions, and seek God's help through prayer. Acknowledge that everyone's situation is unique, but no matter what each person's circumstances may be, money is something everyone can learn more about—how to manage it well, and especially how to manage it according to biblical principles.

Explain the flow of each session. You'll start with a Discussion Starter question or two. Then you'll watch a 13-18 minute video together. That'll be followed by a Group Discussion. You'll end with prayer. There also will be important work to do in between sessions.

Be sure to gather email addresses from all participants so you can be in touch in between sessions.

Within 24 hours of the first meeting, send an email, thanking people for taking part in the study and encouraging them to complete the Take it to Heart and Take Action sections, as well as the Pre-Work for Session 2.

A day or two before Session 2, send another email, reminding group members about the time and location of the next meeting, and encouraging them to be sure to complete the homework from Session 1.

FACILITATING SESSION 2:
MANAGING RISK

The Big Idea

In Session 1, you learned that the stock market's long-term returns have been impressive. However, the ride has not always been smooth; there have been many ups and downs along the way.

Investing always involves risk. This session will highlight four of the most common risks: Inflation risk, longevity risk, market risk, and the risk of getting in your own way. It will then teach participants what they can do to manage each one.

Facilitation Tips

Some of the risks discussed in this session can be managed with practical steps, such as making sure your investment portfolio is adequately diversified. But one of the most significant risks—the risk of getting in your own way—has much to do with more challenging factors, such as patience and fear. Be sure to devote adequate discussion time to the questions that focus on those topics.

As you should every week, send an email to your group within 24 hours after your meeting, thanking people for their participation, and acknowledging anything special that seems worth acknowledging (a helpful direction the conversation went, some encouraging words that were spoken, etc.). Remind people to complete the exercises in the Homework section of the Discussion Guide. And again, send another email a day or two before Session 3, telling the group you're looking forward to the next session, and once again encouraging them to complete the homework.

Make it an important value to have people memorize Scripture each week. As people write God's Word on their hearts and minds, it will powerfully guide them in the wise use of money and help counteract the many unbiblical messages of our culture.

FACILITATING SESSION 3:
THE LEAST TAXING WAY TO INVEST

The Big Idea

We all have a responsibility to pay our taxes. However, taking steps to make sure we don't *overpay* is a part of good stewardship. By using certain investment *vehicles*, such as an IRA or 401(k) plan, we can invest in tax-advantaged ways. This session will help participants decide which of those vehicles may be best for them and then which *type* may be best—a *Traditional* IRA or 401(k) or a *Roth*.

Facilitation Tips

This session is somewhat technical, which may seem confusing to some people. Do your best to engage your group in conversation, reminding them that good stewardship sometimes requires understanding technical material so you can make the best decisions that, in this case, could save on taxes. And besides, God has given each of us a "sound mind" with which we can make such decisions (2 Timothy 1:7).

Keep up the emails this week—send one within 24 hours of your group meeting and another a day or two before Session 4. Encourage people to do the homework and remind them to memorize the memory verse. They should also print and bring the Investing Plan template to Session 4. You may want to bring some extra copies as well since some people may forget.

FACILITATING SESSION 4:
PUTTING IT ALL TOGETHER

The Big Idea

In this session, participants will be taught how to create a written investment plan. Doing so will help them think through their investment goals and investment strategy. They'll also be guided on how to choose specific investments, learning that the key to choosing the right *investments* is choosing the right investment *strategy*.

Remember to bring a few extra copies of the Investment Plan template for anyone who forgets to bring their own.

Facilitation Tips

For this session, some of the most important work will happen *after* your time together. That's when participants will develop a written investment plan and possibly either get started with investing or make some changes to how they're now investing. So, it's important that participants use the group time to really understand how to develop their own investment plan and decide which overall approach to investing they plan to use.

Even though this is the last session, send an email to each participant in the next day or two, thanking them for taking part in the study and seeing if they have any questions. Follow up with them again after a week to check on their progress with Session 4's homework.

Just as you prayed for your group even before your group was formed, it would be very helpful if you would continue to pray for the people in your group. And consider staying in touch in the weeks and months ahead, at least via email, to check in on people, see if they need any further help, and find out more specifically how you could pray for them. You might even want to set up a fifth session four-to-six weeks from now in order to hear about the progress people have made. Some members of your group may want to continue meeting for mutual encouragement and accountability.

Thank you for facilitating this study! We pray that it's been a blessing to you as you've seen the people in your group make progress, and as you've made progress with your own finances as well.

Sound Mind Investing
DIY (With Help)

For more than 25 years, the Sound Mind Investing newsletter has been helping do-it-yourself investors succeed. Our members maintain their own investment accounts at brokers such as Fidelity or Schwab and they make their own trades. But they rely on our objective, time-tested strategies to know what specific mutual funds to invest in.

Multiple Market Beating Strategies

At SMI, we don't make market predictions or recommend investments based on opinion. Instead, all of our strategies rely on a purely objective, rules-based, momentum-driven process. It's a remarkably simple approach that has generated simply remarkable results. See the charts below to compare the growth of $10,000 invested in the stock market versus $10,000 invested in 3 of our most popular strategies. [1]

Sound Mind Investing
Financial Wisdom for Living Well

- THE STOCK MARKET (WILSHIRE 5000): 162% — $26,236
- FUND UPGRADING (SMI STRATEGY): 302% — $40,204
- DAA (SMI STRATEGY): 502% — $60,268
- SECTOR ROTATION (SMI STRATEGY): 1,509% — $160,917

[1] Growth of $10,000 from 2000-2018. DAA and Sector Rotation include results from backtested data.

Sound Mind Investing
HANDBOOK

It's easy to get overwhelmed by all the investing jargon and the many investment options. This clear guide is just the tool you need to become a knowledgeable, confident, successful investor. Join over 100,000 readers who have used the Sound Mind Investing Handbook to learn how to make the most out of what God has entrusted to them.

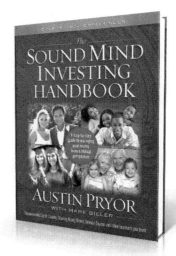

Special Discount Offer
20% Off Retail Price Plus Free Shipping

To learn more, and to take advantage of this special 20% discount, go to:

www.smind.co/handbook

What's Inside

- **Investing Essentials**
  You'll learn the big-picture principles and techniques—the building blocks upon which successful investing plans are constructed. Too many investors focus their learning on specific investments, when in reality, it's mastery of these core principles that usually dictates the success or failure of an investment plan. You'll learn what you *need to know* about investing, not all there is to know.

- **Personalized For You**
  Different people are in different seasons of life and have different comfort levels with risk. You'll take a short, enjoyable investing temperament quiz to assess your risk tolerance. Pairing that with your investing time frame will help you customize an investment portfolio that best meets your unique needs.

- **A Biblical Perspective**
  There's nothing new under the sun (Ecclesiastes 1:9), so you should not be surprised to learn that the underlying values and practical strategies taught in this book are merely the outworkings of concepts taught in God's Word for centuries. Investing in the 21st century, we may be tempted to feel we have grown too sophisticated for biblical lessons. In truth, the complexities and direction of the world point to our need for biblical truth as never before.

- **Clear Language, Not Jargon**
  All of the lessons are worded in everyday "plain-English," and come in small, easy-to-digest portions. Also, you'll find the layout and design of each chapter as clear, interesting, and easy-to-follow as possible.

COMPASS
-finances God's way

Compass- finances God's way is a worldwide, non-profit, interdenominational ministry that teaches people of all ages how to handle money based on the principles of the Bible.

Regardless of where you are on your financial discipleship and generosity journey, Compass will be walking right beside you, giving you the tools and resources you need to be a faithful manager of everything the Lord has entrusted to you.

As you learn and apply what God's word says about handling money, you'll enjoy more financial health, freedom, peace and joy in your life. To get started on your journey we would encourage you to start one of our Small Group Studies or DVD Series.

Small Group Studies

Compass has several life-changing small group studies including; Navigating Your Finances God's Way, Money & Marriage, Business God's Way, Set Your House and Order and our Give, Save & Spend series for college students and teens.

DVD Series

These DVD Studies have been designed to be used in a variety of settings; small groups, seminars, workshops, and even as a self-study. The studies include Navigating Your Finances God's Way, Business God's Way, Money & Marriage God's way and the Give, Save & Spend-Teen Video Series.

"The practical principles in this study are powerful and life-changing because they are based on the Bible. My only regret is that I did not take the course twenty years ago. Don't make the same mistake!"

— Joe Gibbs, Former NFL Head Coach And Founder Of Nascar's Joe Gibbs Racing

To learn more about how to get started on your financial discipleship and generosity journey, please visit us at:

www.compass1.org

50149222R00035

Made in the USA
Columbia, SC
02 February 2019